THE COUPONING BREADCRUMBS

THE HIDDEN SECRETS OF SAVING MONEY USING COUPONS

RUBY FLEURCIUS

The Couponing Breadcrumbs

The Hidden Secrets of Saving Money using Coupons

The Breadcrumb Series Testimonies
Ruby Fleurcius
581 N. Park Ave. Ste. #725
Apopka, FL 32704
321-312-0744

Published in the United States of America

ISBN: 978-1533220509

$14.95

Table of Contents

Dedication

I dedicate this book to my Lord and Savior, who has so dearly blessed me beyond all measure. I also dedicate this book to all of the active and inactive Couponers, and those who are Couponers by occupation or Couponers by hobby, we are one big family; and we deserve to be recognized for our art, perfection of strategy, or our ability to save money. The time that we take to prepare is well worth the money that we save; therefore, we are doing our part in being a good and faithful servant over what You have so dearly blessed us with. I also dedicate this book to all of those who laughed at me when I went out couponing saving my money because surely they are not laughing now. Nevertheless, I believe in the Law of Reciprocity, and I don't mind sharing the same information that got me where I am today. Holy Spirit speak to those who have an open ear and a willing heart to learn how to save through the Art of Couponing. In Jesus name. Amen

Introduction

Are you clipping coupons and finding yourself leaving them at home when you go shopping? Or, better yet, would you like to go from spending $500 a month on groceries to only spending $250 a month?

Who says couponing had to be difficult? If you follow the Couponing Breadcrumb's way of couponing, it will become a piece of cake. I believe that there is no shame in saving money. In my opinion, "If you are not saving money when it's readily available to you—then you should be ASHAMED!"

When we exercise wisdom in the way we are spending our money, we are then better able to become a good steward over other areas of our lives as well. What does saving money on your grocery bill have to do with your lifestyle or way of living? It has everything to do with it. Throwing money away when we don't have to will cause us to become careless and wasteful in other areas of our lives. Nevertheless, if you have it to throw away— couponing is not for you; but, if you are finding yourself living from paycheck to paycheck—it is time for a change. It has been said that we are only 2 paychecks away from being homeless, so why are we spending more on food than we do on our mortgage? Couponing wisdom is one way to save money, and it is also a way to have more of what you could not previously afford to buy.

Couponing Breadcrumb's goal is to teach you how to become a couponing expert! Now, in order to become a Coupon expert yourself, you must:

1. Open your mind to saving money.
2. Change the way you shop.
3. Buy only what's on sale.
4. Look for bargains.
5. Plan what you are going to buy before you go shopping.
6. Shop with confidence as you master the craft of couponing.
7. Learn the average price of the products that you use the most.
8. Build your coupon collection with the Sunday's Paper or Internet Coupons.
9. Get organized.
10. Love Couponing.

In this book you will learn:
1. The purpose of a Coupon.
2. Why people use Coupons.
3. How to use Coupons.
4. Where to find Coupons.
5. Ways to maximize your Coupon usage.

As a Couponing Expert, my ultimate purpose is to give you a better understanding of how to maximize your savings without becoming a victim of impulsive buying. I am going to share the Couponing Breadcrumbs of Wisdom that I accumulated over the past few years. Of course, I don't proclaim to know it all, but what I do know—I am willing to share with you. Today, your journey begins with one step, following the Breadcrumbs that I will place on your path in the right direction.

Chapter 1
Couponing for Life

In today's time, economic hardship has touched individuals and families alike. As a result, we are left scrambling for ways to save money or stretch our dollars as much as possible. As a Couponer, I have found a way to put money back in our pockets by "couponing."

Finding, collecting, and using coupons to save money is difficult for those who do not understand the true art of couponing or how to look for bargains. However, those who take the time to learn how to become a couponer, he or she will begin to enjoy the fruits of their labor by having their cupboard overflowing with products for pennies on the dollar.

As a Coupon Expert, our goal is to shave at least 50-90% off our grocery bill. Yes, it seems impossible; but, very possible for those who become committed to saving money. When I first started couponing, I wasn't an expert, by no means. I was just committed to saving money while helping others to do the same. Now the law of reciprocity has taken over, the more I give—the more I receive. Actually, the best part about my receiving is to receive the wisdom to find the best deals in town. For you, it's not going to happen overnight; it takes time to understand the system and the true value of couponing. By reading this book, it will give you a sense of understanding; however, the best understanding will come when you change the way you think about coupons and when you put your coupon knowledge into practice. Some are afraid or ashamed to use coupons—with me; I am ashamed to pay full price; especially, when I know that I can get a bargain. I changed my whole mindset about the way I buy products—it's in my blood now, and my pantry is overflowing. I have more than enough and some to give away.

One of the most important keys to couponing is to keep an open mind with the product brands. In so many words, flexibility is required to become a master at couponing. Instead of saving 4 or 5 dollars when checking out, we can slash our grocery bill 25-50% within a month of using this couponing system. Once we become well-versed in using coupons, it will become 50-90% as long as we do not get stuck using one brand of product. If we do, we will miss out on some great bargains, to say the least. "WHAT" we purchase may change from time to time—it's "HOW" we purchase products that make the big difference. The recession is indeed driving people to utilize coupons more often. Believe it or not, there are coupons available that will cater to most of our needs and it's our job to find them. Coupons are not just for food—there is a coupon out there for almost everything. Listed below is a breakdown of the percentage of coupons that are out there waiting to fulfill our different needs:

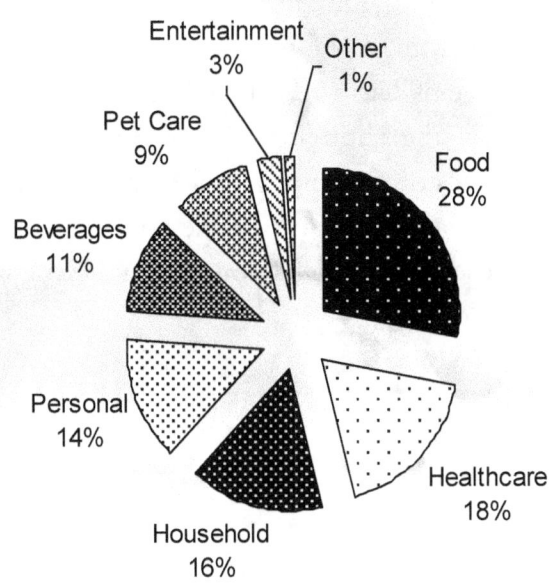

Just look around you. Coupons are everywhere. 28% of all the coupons in the world are for food items. 18% are for Healthcare, medicines, etc. 16% are for household & cleaning items. 14% are for personal & hygiene items.

11% are for beverages, 9% are for Pets, 3% are for entertainment & restaurants, and 1% is for other. Whatever you need, I am pretty sure that there is a coupon for it—you just have to take the time to look for it.

There is so much money that we can save that we are just giving away because we lack the understanding of how much we can actually save on simple items that we use every day. Nevertheless, I am going to leave a Trail of Breadcrumbs that's going to make it very easy and simple to do, even with a full-time job. I understand that couponing seems like a tedious job, and it could be if we do not know the shortcuts. Therefore, I am going to teach the basics of couponing, and I am going to teach the short-cuts as well. This will enable you to coupon for life and pass these Breadcrumbs down to the next generation.

Chapter 2

Couponing Breadcrumbs Rules

Even the wisest person has something that he or she can learn and if we want to find or even save money—it's in our shopping cart. The money we should be saving, we are giving away. Coupons are real money that we overlook on a daily basis. As our budgets get tighter, we must find ways to cut back or save money, and I have found that using coupons is one way to do so. I read that there are over 300 billion dollars in coupons that go unused every year. Yes, over 300 billion dollars that we as consumers, overlook every year. I know for a fact that we can benefit from some of that money—we may not get it all, but I am devoted to doing my part to help others benefit from what we have taken for granted.

The very first time I used coupons, I was very nervous; however, I did save $40.00. I was so proud of myself that

I began to share my experience with everyone who would listen to me. Even though some may say that saving $40.00 wasn't a lot of money, but for me—it was a bargain. Now, I am addicted to couponing. Of course, most people look at couponers as if they are living below the poverty line; but I must say that it's so far from the truth. It's not the individuals with a limited income that are using the bulk of the coupons; it is the middle and upper-class individuals. As a matter of fact, I often wondered why those who make less money pay full price for their groceries. After doing my homework, I understand why—it is the lack of understanding. My goal as a Coupon Expert is to teach everyone, the rich, the poor and anyone in between, how to cut their grocery bill in half and give you some Breadcrumbs of WISDOM that will keep a few dollars in your pocket. In doing so, I do have a few rules:

1. Make a decision to save as much money as possible.

2. Decide on your favorite stores to shop and get their coupon policy. Here in Central Florida, I shop at Publix, Wal-Mart, Albertsons, Winn-Dixie, Walgreens, CVS, Dollar General, Dollar Tree, and Target. Of course, there are more stores, but these are the 9 stores that I focus on. Depending on where you live, there is Aldi, Bi-Lo, Food Lion, Fred Meyer, Fry's, Giant Eagle, Harris Teeter,

Kmart, Kroger, Meijer, Ralphs, Rite Aid, Safeway/Vons, Shop-Rite, Smiths, or Whole Foods, you need to pick your favorite stores, master their coupon policy and save some real money.

3. Get the Sunday's Paper for coupons or get your coupons online. You are allowed to print 2 coupons per computer. It will serve you well to have more than 1 computer. Word of Caution: Do not copy internet coupons—they can be traced back to your computer. Coupon Fraud is a Felony; each coupon has a different number and security features; it can be easily tracked back to your IP address. If you are going to become a great couponer, make sure you do the right thing— do not copy the coupon, it affects everyone and not just yourself. If you desire a lot of coupons, buy more of the Sunday's Paper or purchase them from a coupon clipping service.

4. Use a laser printer, preferably in black & white to print internet coupons. It's cheaper than using an inkjet color printer. Besides, you don't want to invest all of the money you save in buying ink cartridges every couple of weeks.

5. Pick up all of your local in-store ads and in-store coupons, or you are now able to use your smart mobile device to download coupons.

6. Do not use your personal email address to sign up for coupons. Set up a different email account to receive your coupons and/or special offers for digital coupons.

7. Do not cut out all the coupons—it takes up too much of your time. With the Couponing Breadcrumb's system, there is no need to cut out every coupon. Only cut out what you need to eliminate the coupon clutter, write the date on each coupon insert and place it in your Coupon Binder or Coupon File. When you find an item that's a bargain for you—go to your binder or file pull out the coupon or print the coupon, put it on your shopping list, attach the coupon and go shopping. Most often you will never use the coupon until there is a BARGAIN. That means that you may have to sit on coupons until that item goes on sale. Trust me, when there is a high dollar coupon for a certain item, the stores will intentionally put that item on sale to round up that coupon! I need you to spend more time on researching your bargains than you spend on cutting coupons—you are not a coupon cutter! I need you to search for your Breadcrumbs and order your coupons in advance if

necessary. That means that you need to prepare and plan your deals before the sale ends.

8. Never shop when you are depressed, angry, hungry, or tired. This creates impulsive buys that may sabotage your efforts to save money. Eat, relax, calm yourself down or get yourself in a better mood before you shop! Trust me, shopping on a full stomach with a clear mind has saved me thousands of dollars.

9. Take your calculator with you and calculate your bill as you go. Don't forget to deduct your coupons as well—this will give you an idea of how much you will be paying before you get to the register.

10. Get more than one set of coupons. Buy more than one Sunday's paper, buy them off eBay, buy them from a coupon clipping service, or exchange coupons on Facebook with your friends and family members.

11. Stack coupons as much as possible. The goal is to use multiple coupons on one product, especially on the true BOGO items. A **true** BOGO item is when you buy an item at full price, and you get the next item free. A **non-true** BOGO is when an

item is advertised as BOGO, but rings up at the register as half-price for each item.

12. Learn how to plan, eat, and prepare your meals based on what's on sale. The Golden Rule is to "eat what's on sale." This is challenging in the beginning, but once you become accustomed to it, you will thank me!

13. Buy what you need. Do not buy items just because you have a coupon for it, unless you are getting it for pennies on the dollar or for FREE.

14. Take the time to research sales ads, organize your coupons, and make a shopping list. Organization is one tool that's going to help you save a lot of time—without it, you are going to have a mess!

15. Become flexible with the brands to ensure that you are able to get the best bargain.

16. Read your coupons carefully to ensure that you get the right items.

17. Get a rain check if the sale item is out of stock.

18. Get the coupon policy of the store you shop at.

19. If a store has a problem with you using coupons in their store—GO TO ANOTHER STORE. There are other stores that would be glad to accept your coupons with no problem.

20. When you get to the register, give the cashier your coupons last. This way you are able to watch them deduct every coupon to ensure that you don't miss a coupon, and that you do not get confused about what's being deducted from your bill.

21. Read your ads every week to see what's on sale. If possible, preview your sales ads early.

22. Do your coupon matchups or price-match before you go shopping. This will better prepare you to learn how to buy what's on sale or what you can get for a bargain. Please use a matchup cheat sheet —do not overwork yourself. Keep it simple; the work is already done for you. Go to these websites, click on your store link, and go over the current in-store ad. The ad will tell you what coupons you need to print, and which coupon that you will need to order, or which coupon you will need from Redplum or Smartsource. Between these 2 websites, you will be able to find all the stores in your area regardless of where you live in the United States. Here are the sites: The 1st website is the most user-friendly.

www.thekrazycouponlady.com
www.southersavers.com

23. Make a shopping list. This list will keep you on track to ensure that you do not forget what you went to the store for; and, it keeps you from buying what you don't need or have a coupon for.

24. Do not clear the shelves when shopping. Be courteous, you are not the only person looking for a deal.

25. Your time is valuable. Don't waste it!

26. Keep track of how much you are spending, know your budget, and how much you are saving.

27. Don't feel bad about holding up the line, your money is important!

If you have a desire to become a professional couponer, it's not going to come to you by luck; it's going to come to you by skill. What that means is that you are going to have to practice, practice, and practice some more, until it becomes second nature.

Chapter 3

Smart Ways of Couponing

Couponers are often laughed at, when they should be commended for saving money. The commitment to saving money is not a laughing matter; especially when it's readily available to us. There are so many different ways to save money, but for the purpose of this book, we are going to stick to saving money through couponing. As the economy becomes very challenging, it's our responsibility to consider other effective money saving options. I have heard since childhood that a penny saved is a penny earned. Just remember those pennies add up to dollars, those dollars will become hundreds and eventually thousands as we make a difference in the way we live, the way we think, and the choices that we make in our everyday life.

As a couponer, don't allow anyone to stop you from saving money. I have had people behind me at the checkout counter smirk, crack jokes and even get mad at me for trying to save money—which is something they should be doing as well. But, when they noticed that I am only paying a few dollars or saving hundreds of dollars before their very eyes, you should see how quick that smirk or anger becomes admiration. Let me explain something; it does not take a rocket scientist to understand that coupons are like real money, and it's not a game. It is wise to use a coupon in order to save your currency for other important things such as:

1. Spending quality time with your family.
2. Taking your family on vacation.
3. A new home.
4. A new car.
5. Debt reduction.
6. Emergency Fund.
7. Starting a new business.
8. Living your dream.
9. Donating to your favorite charity.

The list goes on, but you have to decide what you are going to do with the extra money that you save on your grocery bill. I have found that the best way to keep up with what you are saving is to keep a log book. Every time you save any money, just write it down—this is a good way to give you more of an incentive to keep the money that you are giving away at your local grocer; and, it will help keep you focused on your ultimate goal of saving money.

As we get back on the subject, every coupon is not a good deal, and every item that goes on sale is not always a bargain; therefore, we must know our prices. We must take the time to understand the difference between a bargain and getting a discount. As a Coupon Expert, WE LOOK FOR BARGAINS! A bargain is considered 50-90% off the retail price. A discount is 20-40% off the retail price. We sometimes settle for the 40% off, but our ultimate goal is the find name-brand bargains 50-90% off. As a Coupon Expert, we do not consider generic branded products a bargain. We are not degrading generic products; however, when using coupons, usually the generic products cost more than the brand-name products.

The best bargains usually occur when an item goes on sale, and we are able to combine or stack our coupons. For example: 1 manufacturer's coupon with 1 in-store coupon, 1 manufacturer's coupon with 1 Competitors coupon, 1 manufacturer's coupon with a price match, or 2 manufacturer's/in-store coupons on a BOGO item. If I just confused you, I will explain this process in detail in another chapter.

Coupon Organization
The best way to organize your coupons is by the product categories such as dairy, deli, detergent, meats, snacks, etc.

Then sort coupons by the date of expiration so that you are able to discard the expired coupons quickly and efficiently. I have found that if you store your coupons in a binder, envelopes, file wallet, or index file box, you are able to stay organized and save time as well. One way of organization will not work for everyone—you will have to find what works for you and develop your own system. Therefore, it will eliminate excuses such as:

1. I don't have enough time.
2. I forgot my coupons at home.
3. My coupon has expired.
4. I can't keep up.
5. I am too busy.
6. Couponing overwhelms me.
7. I can't find any good deals.
8. I rather pay full price.

We are not just focused on saving money; we are focused on saving time as well. Time is money, and if we are saving money, then we can't waste time! As a Coupon Expert "Going with the flow" or "winging it" are not in our vocabulary! When a Couponer enters a store, we go in with a plan! We must have our shopping list in hand, along with our pulled coupons. Of course, we will have our backup coupons in the car, just in case we find items on clearance. For the most part, we prepare in advance to save money.

Break through the coupon Hoax

The stores expect us to jump over dollars to save a nickel. In so many words, we bring a few coupons worth $5.00 in savings and walk out of their store spending more than we came to save. I've done it. As a matter of fact, we've all done it—we go to the store for one thing and come out with several things that we did not anticipate buying; therefore, spending more and saving less. However, our goal is to reverse the role; we need to start saving more and spending less by breaking through the hoax that the stores and the manufacturer's set for us. The stores expect the inexperienced couponers to come into their stores to:

1. Misuse or misread their coupons.
2. Buy what they don't need.
3. Stock up on groceries that they did not come to buy.
4. SPEND MORE MONEY.

The manufacturers put out coupons for a few reasons:

1. To entice you to buy their product.
2. To get you to try a new product.
3. Rejuvenate your loyalty.
4. To increase sales.
5. To sell products that are about to expire.
6. To move discontinued products off the shelf.
7. To make good on a previously recalled product.
8. To simply get the couponers to clean the shelf.

From now on, when you walk into a store, your ultimate goal is to save money! When that mindset is developed, you will begin to start looking at your purchases differently. This is not a matter of being cheap; it's a matter of maximizing your potential to save money through the use of coupons. Don't get caught up in the impulsive buying frenzy—stores will place products in the aisles to cause you to buy items you think you need while you are on your way to the essential items, such as milk, bread, soda, water, etc. Most often, the essential items will always be located in the back of the store. The store wants to entice you to unknowingly walk through the store to pick up items before you get to what you really need.

Impulsive Buying

Procter & Gamble is one company that believes in putting out coupons—they have targeted the market with their monthly coupon insert. As a matter of fact, a once failing company has now made billions by offering coupons to consumers for pharmaceutical supplies, cleaning supplies, personal care, and pet supplies. P & G is a marketing giant, and it's their job to create impulsive buying—they make billions on those who only buy their product because they had a coupon for it. Just because you have a coupon for an item does not mean that you have to run out and buy it. Impulsive buying for a couponer is a big No-No, unless it's FREE or almost free! Sampling products in the store is a big No-No as well. A true couponer needs to exercise DISCIPLINE when shopping! Yes, P & G will make their money their way, and you will learn to save your money by purchasing bargains your way.

A store's ultimate goal is to get you to spend money, and your ultimate goal is to save money. This thought process is not what stores want us to have—so they will try to make it difficult for those who really know how to use coupons. In so many words, they don't worry about the inexperience couponer—that's their **MONEY-MAKER**. However, they worry about the real couponers who know and understand what they are doing and the reasons why. To me, giving away money is not a good enough reason for me to allow impulsive buying to control my ability to save money. My goal is to save money and in order for me to stay on track—I must plan what I am going to buy. I do not deviate from my shopping list unless it's a real good bargain or an emergency product that I need right away. Other than that, stick to the plan, and not fall victim to the impulsive buying syndrome.

Chapter 4

Learning the Language

Most often people redeem coupons by the picture located on the coupon, and when they get to the register, it's the wrong product—they can't use the coupon, but they get the product anyway. Manufacturers will go to the extreme of putting a picture of the most expensive product on the coupon to trick us; therefore, we must read the coupon carefully. Now with Couponing Breadcrumbs, that's totally unacceptable—we interpret coupons by the wording, not the picture. For this reason, it's imperative that we learn the coupon language of a Couponer. Read the coupon before it's redeemed to ensure that you are purchasing the right product, as well as the right amount of product. I have listed a few terms to help you learn the Coupon Lingo:

$1.00/1, $2.00/1: The first number represents the discount and the second number indicates the quantity required to obtain that discount. For example: One dollar off one product, two dollars off one product, etc.

$1.00/2, $2.00/2: The first number represents the discount and the second number indicates the quantity required to obtain that discount. For example: you will receive one dollar off two products, or two dollars off two products. You cannot redeem the coupon on one product—it's imperative that you purchase 2 items to use your coupon.

Addy: Address

AR: After Rebate

BOGO: Buy one, get one free.

B1G1, B2G1: This also means buy one, get one free. The "B" represents "buy", the G represents "get". The numbers designate how many of a product you must buy in order to qualify and the number of products you acquire when you redeem the coupon or offer. For example: B1G1= Buy one, get one free. B2G1= Buy two, get one free. B2G2= Buy two, get two free.

Blinkie: This is the coupon machine that dispenses manufacturer coupons, it is usually found on grocery aisles next to the product. This is often recognized by a blinking red light. The machine basically dispenses the coupon one at a time. These coupons can be redeemed at any store that accepts coupons. So, stock up when you can.

BOLO: Be on the Lookout

BOOKLET: Manufacturer's Coupon mail-out pamphlet

C/O: Cents-Off Coupons

Catalina or CAT: This is a little machine located at the checkout register that dispenses manufacturer or store coupons that may be used on your next purchase. The coupons for money off your next purchase or money off a specific item can be used as a competitor's coupon as well. You will be surprised at how much you can save when you keep up with the discounts on your register receipts. Most often, you will find them at Walgreens and Winn-Dixie.

Closeouts: Is when a store does not plan on re-stocking an item. This is a great time to use your coupons as well. Always check the clearance racks before leaving the store—you may have a coupon for an item that's greatly reduced anyway. HINT: this is a great way to get free items.

Competitors: Are stores are carrying similar products that compete for your business. Some grocery stores or drug stores will take other grocery or drug store's coupons in order to keep your business. As a rule of thumb, always check the couponing policy at each store and find out which stores they consider a competitor. As a matter of fact, Publix Supermarket is the only store I know that takes competitor coupons.

Couponing Policy: Each store has their own set of guidelines to follow when using coupons. And it is your responsibility to find out their policy to ensure that you are able to maximize your coupon usage without wasting your time.   Find out whether they take competitor's coupons, "double" or "triple" coupons, accept Internet coupons or if they even accept coupons at all.

Coupon Insert: This is basically the coupon circulars inserted into the Sunday's newspaper. Most often you will find a packet of Source (SS), Red Plum (RP) or Proctor and Gamble (PG) coupons.

Coupon: Is a clipping from a store or manufacturer that entitles a shopper to a discount on specific products. The best way to get these clippings is to pick up the Sunday's Newspaper   or   print   them   from   Coupons.com, SmartSource.com, RedPlum.com, Target.com or the manufacturer's website.

Couponing: This is the practice of redeeming discount coupons in order to save money.

Couponer: A person who collects and saves coupons to redeem them on products, such as groceries or HBA (Health and Beauty Aid) items.

CPN: Coupon

CRT: Cash Register Tape is basically your receipt. Usually, this is referred to CVS coupons that print at the bottom of your receipt. It's usually based on your purchase history.

DD: Dumpster Diving

DND: Do Not Double

Double Coupons: Certain stores double coupons up to a certain value, usually $0.50. Some stores may also set a maximum value limit; however, in Florida coupon doubling is very rare, but possible.

Ea: Each.

ECB or Extra Bucks: Extra Bucks is exclusively at CVS Stores. This coupon prints at the end of your receipts—it's basically cash toward your next order.

E-Coupons: Electronic coupons may be downloaded onto your store loyalty card or cell phone. At Target, you can download a coupon using the mobile apps and show your discount code to your cashier. It's just that easy.

ETS: Excludes trial size.

EXP: Expires or Expiration Date.

ES: Easy Saver. This is a monthly rebate and coupon book at Walgreens. You can stack them with manufacturer coupons at Walgreens.

FAR: Free After Rebate.

Filler Item: An item used to meet the minimum coupon requirement to use a certain amount of coupons. This is usually used at Walgreens. You are able to stack coupons at Walgreens, but their system will only allow 1 coupon per product. For every item that you use 2 coupons on, you need a filler item for it. I use a .33 cent piece of candy or a very cheap item as my filler item.

GC: Gift card.

GM: General Mills

Internet Printable or IP : A coupon that can be printed online.

IVC: Instant Value Coupon at Walgreens

MIR: Mail in Rebate, refers to rebates which must be submitted by mail. These are the traditional rebates that require you to mail in both your receipt and proof of purchase in the form of UPC barcodes.

MFR or MFG: Manufacturer (The Company that produces a certain item.)

MIR: Mail-in Rebate

MM: Money Maker. This is where you receive an overage on a product after redeeming a coupon or coupon(s). Some stores are not allowed to give you money back, some stores like Wal-Mart will give you money back, and some stores allow your overage to carryover to other items that you are purchasing.

MQ: Manufacturer's Coupon. This is a discount coupon offered by the Manufacturer or Marketing Company that offers a discount to entice you to buy or sample their product. When a coupon is redeemed, the manufacturer will then reimburse the store for the entire value of the coupon, plus a handling fee.

NED: No Expiration Date

NLA: No longer Available.

OAS: On Any Size

OOP: Out-of-Pocket. This is the amount of money you will pay the store for your products.

OOS: Out of Stock

OYNO or OYNSO: On Your Next Order or On Your Next Shopping Order. For example, a store promotion will be: spend $50.00, save $5.00 on your next order.

One Coupon per Purchase: Is one coupon per item. This means that you cannot use 2 like coupons for the same item.

One Coupon per Transaction: Limits you to only using one coupon per transaction. Just ask to do separate transactions.

Peelie: This is the peel-off coupon found on product packaging. Please read the fine print before you try to redeem the coupon when checking out. Some manufacturers bank on you not reading the coupon properly.

P&G: Proctor & Gamble. They are one of the largest corporations in the world. Proctor and Gamble put out a monthly coupon inserts filled with coupons for a variety of Proctor and Gamble products.

PM: Price Match or Private Message

POP: Proof of Purchase

Purchase: Is simply buying an item. If you buy 20 items on a single shopping trip, you will have made 20 purchases in one transaction.

Q: Is the abbreviation commonly used to refer to a coupon.

Rain Check or RC: When a store is out of a sale item, a rain check is written to allow you to get the sale price whenever the item comes back in stock. If you have a coupon for it—GET YOUR RAINCHECK! Go to the customer service desk to request your rain check for the out of stock product. On certain items, it will specifically say, "No rainchecks" and some stores will put an expiration date on their rainchecks. Regardless of what it says, HINT: Do not wait until the last minute to do your bargain shopping, start early to ensure that you are able to maximize your coupons.

Rebate: A rebate is a refund of part or the entire amount paid.

RR: Register Rewards. This is done exclusively at Walgreens.   They work like cash on your next order with certain restrictions.

Rolling Catalinas: Is basically separating your purchase into multiple transactions in order to maximize your Catalina coupons.   For example, you use the Catalina coupon from your first transaction to pay for your second transaction, then another Catalina coupon prints from the 2nd transaction that pays for the 3rd transaction and so on.

RP: Red Plum coupon inserts come in your local paper. Their website features a variety of coupons from certain manufacturers that can be printed right from your computer.

SCR or Single Check Rebate: This is Rite Aid Drugstore's monthly rebate program. Each month you simply pick up your rebate booklet to receive hundreds of dollars in savings.

SS: Smart Source is part of News America Marketing Co. Smart Source coupon inserts can be found in most Sunday's papers and on their website as well.

Stacking: When you use two promotions together, it is often referred to as stacking. This is the term that is often used when stores will let you use a store coupon or competitor's coupon along with a manufacturer's coupon for the same item. This is where you find the bargains! In Florida, the best stores to stack your coupons are Publix, Target, Winn-Dixie, Albertsons, Walgreens and CVS.

Stockpile or SP: Is to buy many items at a time in order to build your stockpile or stash of food and non-food items. In so many words STOCKUP!

Store Coupon: Is an in-store coupon created by a particular store to entice you to buy a certain product. Stores do not get reimbursed for an in-store or competitor's coupon. This is where you will find the bargains if you learn how to stack coupons—so make sure you check the store's weekly ad or monthly promotions.

Store Loyalty Card: This is a free card which you present at checkout to receive additional discount or savings.

Transaction: a transaction refers to your total order, regardless of how many items you have.

Tear Pad or TP: This is a pad of coupons located near the product on shopping aisles that you simply tear off.

WAGS: Is the abbreviation for Walgreens.

W/L: Wish List

UPC: Universal bar Code. This is the bar code that stores use to electronically scan products for pricing and inventory purposes. And it is also used for mail-in rebates as well.

WYB: When You Buy. Some sales or coupons require you to purchase multiple items, so read the coupon very carefully before you checkout.

YMMV: Your Mileage May Vary. This is a phrase used to describe the experience of a particular shopper, who finds a deal but they want you to know that your store branch may not offer the same deal.

Once you truly understand how to read coupons, you are able to put the ball in your court; especially, when you start racking up on bargains for pennies on the dollar.

Chapter 5

Getting the Coupon Fever

Your ultimate goal is never to pay full price again. I have found that saving money is just as addictive as spending it; however, with Couponing Breadcrumbs, our goal is to save money period! Once you learn this system of using coupons, you will never want for anything—you will always have the best, up-to-date products on the market. Now, in order to do so, you must learn a few things:

1. Your prices.
2. That sales run in a 6-8 week cycle.
3. Where to find coupons.
4. How to read a coupon.
5. How to use a coupon.
6. What's considered a deal?

How to use coupons

For the beginners, a manufacturer's coupon is a coupon that clearly states "Manufacturer's Coupon" on it. All manufacturer coupons will have a scannable bar code that reveals the amount of savings you will receive. Stores will not accept a manufacturer's coupon without a bar code or expiration date.

UCC Company Prefix is considered to be the Manufacturer's ID. This number helps verify that you are purchasing the right product for the right coupon

Family Code is the Manufacturers way of creating several different product lines under one umbrella. Basically, they break down their product lines into families to enable coupons to validate on the right brand of product.

Value Code is a number that tells the register what you need to purchase and how much to deduct.

Check Digit is for the scanner. This number makes sure that it has read the correct numbers for the correct product.

A manufacturer's coupon will also have a mailing address listed for the retailer to use similar to this:

Consumer: This coupon good at retail outlets only and on products indicated. One coupon per purchase. You must pay any sales tax. Void if reproduced, altered, transferred, exchanged, sold or purchased. Good only in U.S.A. and Puerto Rico, except where prohibited, taxed or restricted by law. Cash value1/100¢. Retailer: Mountain Grain will reimburse you for the face value plus 8¢ handling if submitted in compliance with our redemption policy. Copies available upon request. For reimbursement, mail to: Mountain Grain, CMS Department #20, One Laffurry Drive, Del Rio, TX 78841.

Now that you understand what type of information that's listed on a manufacturer's coupon, here is an actual coupon:

The Couponing Breadcrumbs

This coupon is designed to give a discount for a specified product that can be redeemed at any store that carries that specific product and accepts coupons. **We are allowed to use 1 manufacturer's coupon per indicated items purchased—we cannot use 2 manufacturer coupons on 1 product.** In order to receive a discount or a percentage off, you must purchase the product specified on the coupon or fulfill the requirements of the coupon. For example, if the coupon states that you need to purchase 3 bottles of water in order to receive a $1 off— you would need to buy 3 bottles of waters to get $1 off. The cashier will scan the coupon; then you pay the difference—it's just that simple. Make sure you double-check the expiration date to ensure that the coupon hasn't expired.

As we move on, once we understand how to use a manufacturer's coupon—now we must understand the value of an in-store coupon. An in-store coupon is a coupon from the store that they do not get reimbursed for, but we are allowed to use an in-store coupon along with a manufacturer's coupon to maximize our savings. Yes, we are allowed to use 1 in-store coupon and 1 manufacturer's coupon together for the same item. Please double-check the store's coupon policy to ensure that they allow the stacking of coupons on a specific product.

One manufacturer's coupon per item, period! You cannot use 2 manufacturer coupons on one item. *(You cannot save up your manufacturer coupons for one item and use them all at one time on that one item—you must have a separate* *manufacturer's coupon for each item.)* The best way to remember this is to count your manufacturer coupons before you get to the register. If you have more manufacturer coupons than the items that you are purchasing—something's wrong. However, when you are stacking manufacturer coupons with an in-store or competitor coupon, the in-store or competitor coupon should never exceed the amount of products as well. For example, if you purchase 20 items—you cannot have more than 20 manufacturer coupons and 20 in-store or competitor coupons, if the store allows stacking. If they do not allow stacking (using a manufacturer's coupon + an in-store or competitor's coupon), you cannot have more than 20 manufacturer's coupon for the 20 items that are being purchased. Here's an example of how to stack coupons at target for Huggies diapers:

Manufacturer's Coupon

In-store Coupon

If the diapers cost 12.99 minus a $2.00 manufacturer's coupon minus a $3.00 off in-store coupon = you pay 7.99 plus tax. Stacking coupons is really easy once you get the hang of it.

Publix Supermarket, a company out of Lakeland, Florida is the only store that accepts competitor's coupons. If your local Publix accepts competitor's coupons from Target—you can take these same coupons over to their store and receive the same coupon privilege. However, Publix has cracked down on who they consider a competitor—so, check with your local store before attempting to use competitor coupons.

In the Central Florida area some Publix locations are taking competitor coupons from:

1. Winn-Dixie
2. Albertsons
3. Target
4. Save-a-lot

5. Fresh Market
6. Whole Foods

Each Publix location may vary due to the competitors within a 5-mile radius. I have found that Publix is a little biased in who they consider a competitor based on the amount of couponers in that particular area. The more couponers Publix have in a particular area, the more they limit quantities, and the more they give their professional couponers a hard time because some couponers tend to abuse their privileges. When using competitor coupons, Publix is very adamant about the product being the exact same product or brand listed on the coupon; especially on BOGO meat products that are usually found in the Albertson's sales ad. Since Albertsons jack their prices up on the offer a B1G2, Publix will only honor that particular coupon as a B1G1. If you are in doubt about whether or not you are able to use a coupon for a particular brand or cut of meat, simply ask the meat manager. This will help avoid any type of confusion when you check out.

Walgreens will allow you to use a manufacturer coupon along with an in-store coupon; however, if you have 20 coupons (manufacturer's or in-store) you must have the same amount of items. For example, I have 5 items in my cart, and I have 5 manufacturer coupons and 1 in-store coupon, totaling 6 coupons. I must have a filler item, to bring my total up to 6 items. This is Walgreen's way of getting you to buy what you don't need in order to save money.

Where to find Coupons

Most often you will find coupons in the Sunday's paper, magazines, grocery stores, drug stores, the internet, cellphone/smartphones, mailers, All You Magazine in Wal-Mart and in-store promotional booklets. You will also find coupons on "peelies" attached to the product, pads of coupons on store displays, store flyers, and email subscriptions. The use of the internet has provided a forum that would allow us to print coupons from Twitter, FaceBook, websites, and blogs. You can also just print your coupons from SmartSource.com, RedPlum.com, Coupons.com, Target.com, Valpak.com, the store's website, or the manufacturer's website.

When looking for coupons, simply go to Thekrazycouponlady.com or SouthernSavers.com database to see if there is a coupon for the product(s) that you are looking for. If there is a coupon out there, log on to that website and print the coupon.

If you want to make it easy for yourself, order your coupons from eBay.com, CollectableCoupons.com, TheCouponClippers.com, CouponFleaMarket.com, or join a group who trade coupons on Facebook, or create your own group Facebook to trade coupons.

Stockpile

Stockpiling is basically stocking up. Of course, you are going to need more than just 2 or 3 coupons to stockpile. Do you have to buy a lot of Sunday's papers to get the coupons? Yes, you can; but, you don't have to—just order your coupons from CollectableCoupons.com, eBay.com, CouponFleaMarket.com or TheCouponClippers.com. However, when ordering coupons from a clipping service, order them early to ensure that you don't miss out on the sale.

Buying in larger quantities when you find a bargain is definitely the way to go. You will find that stockpiling will help save you money on things that you are going to use. For example, your family consumes 2 boxes of cereal a week, and you found a bargain that would allow you to purchase 2 boxes for the price of one. One box is normally $3.99, and with this sale you are able to purchase each box for $2.00. That's your time to stock up. When a product goes on sale, preferably BOGO, you want to buy enough of it to last until it goes on sale again. This deal would become even better if you have coupons on top of the sale price. For example: Each box is $2.00 and you have 2 manufacturer coupons for $1.00 off, you will then pay $1.00 for each box. So, watch out for the BOGO items—that's where you are going to find the best deals. You are allowed to use a manufacturer's coupon on each item and one in-store coupon for each item as well. Better yet, if a store is running a true BOGO sale (not a half-off sale) and you have a BOGO coupon—you are able to use that as well. For example, with a BOGO item, the store is paying for one, and you have to pay for the other item, plus tax. If you have a BOGO coupon, the store pays for 1 item, the manufacturer pays for the other item and you simply pay the tax. If a particular store does not allow you to use your BOGO coupon on a BOGO item, don't fight with them, just go to another store.

When stocking up, make sure you are paying the lowest price possible and that you have a coupon or coupons for it. By the way, purchasing the item in smaller sizes will tend to be a lot cheaper than purchasing the larger size item, unless it's on sale. As a word of caution, some stores will increase the price of a product and then offer a coupon to make you think that you are getting a deal when you are not. For that reason, you must know your prices. This is one aspect of couponing will prove to be very valuable; especially when you are price matching or doing a price comparison. You will find that the more you save, the more you are able to buy—just make sure you check the expiration date on each item before stocking up on it. We must pay attention to the shelf life to ensure that what you are stocking up on is not going to go bad anytime soon.

The items can be stored in your garage, basement, shed or storage room; and, of course, the extra freezer items can be stored in a deep freezer.

Overage
"Overage" means that the value of a coupon exceeds the price of the item. Example: my coupon is for $2 off any Kellogg's cereal, but the cereal is on sale for $1.75. This results in a .25¢ overage. Many stores allow you to apply the overage to the rest of your order because the store

gets reimbursed for the full value of the coupon plus an 8¢ handling fee. If you see an item on sale that is free "plus overage," buy as many of that item as you have coupons! Use your coupon overage for items that don't often have coupons such as: milk, bread, meat, produce, and so on. Even if you don't need the item, you probably know someone who does, and it takes money off of the rest of your groceries.

Some stores will not allow overage and some will. Find the stores that will and shop there.

Common Misunderstanding

When reading a coupon the phrase stating, "**one per purchase**" means that you are able to use one coupon per item being purchased. Basically, each item, no matter how many you have, is a purchase—unless the coupon has a specific limit. For example: "**Limit 4 like Coupons**," which means you can only use 4 of the same coupons. You will find that a lot of cashiers will misunderstand these phrases—so, you must be on your P's and Q's. However, if your coupon says, "**one per transaction**," it means that you are only able to use one coupon for that item for your entire transaction, regardless of how many of the same items that you are purchasing. FYI, some stores will allow you to do separate transactions, as long as it doesn't say "**one per visit**" or "**one per customer**."

From my experience, most corporate policies state that every time you walk into a store, you are a "new" customer. If you do not have time to go to another store, take the products from your first transaction out to your car, go back into the store to continue shopping and go to a different cashier.

Once you are able to master some of these simple principles, you will find that you are better able to shop with confidence.

Chapter 6

Shop with Confidence

Saving money is the way to go. If you have money to throw away, then keep throwing it away—the stores are catching those dollars, and that's why they are still in business. A smart shopper is a shopper worthy of his or her savings.

Always remain calm, even if you get a hellion as a cashier—be kind to them. If a store dislikes or hassles you, go to another store. There are other stores that would gladly accept your coupons without giving you a hassle.

Pay attention

In order for me to become a pro at couponing, I had to develop a system that worked for me. As I began to work my system without deviation, I became more confident in couponing until the cashiers began to recognize that I knew more about coupons than they did. I have also found that if some cashier realizes that you don't know what you are doing, they will try to prevent you from using certain coupons or saving money. Besides, most cashiers hate coupons, unless they are a couponer themselves. So, I make it my business to watch everything. Before I check out, I follow this process:

1. I count all of my coupons.
2. I double-check to see if I have the right amount of items.
3. I place my items on the counter/belt in order, according to the coupons I have in my hand.
4. I let the cashier scan all of the items.
5. I hand her the coupons for each item as I watch the item being deducted.
6. I use my $ off coupon first. For example: at Publix, I use my $5.00 off $30.00 coupon first.
7. I give the cashier my BOGO Coupons. If I have a lot of BOGO coupons, I will put the coupon with the item to save the cashier some time. If you do not, your cashier will have to go back to find the price of the item, which is very time consuming if they are new.
8. I give them the manufacturer's coupon and the in-store or competitor's coupon for each product. **FYI:** At Walgreens, always give them the manufacturer's coupon before you give them the store coupon.

9. Before I leave the store, I look at my receipt, and count the amount of coupons that should have been taken off.

This process helps me to keep track of the coupons that are being scanned. I have found that when I give my coupons to the cashier ahead of time—there have been several coupons missed; therefore, it takes me more time to find the mistake and to get my money back. Some would say, "What's the big deal if they missed 1 coupon?" For me, it's a big deal—if I visit 4 stores in one week and each store missed a coupon worth $1.00 each, that's $4.00 a week, $16.00 a month, $192 a year. Those dollars add up—I am in this business to save money and every dollar counts! Our coupons are like real money; don't feel ashamed to ask for your money back.

Food Stamps/EBT

Those who are receiving food stamps/EBT or SNAP are able to use coupons with their purchases as well. Coupons are a form of payment; however, when using your EBT or card, you may be subject to paying the tax on the coupon depending on where you shop. When using your EBT/SNAP card with coupons, DO NOT purchase non-food items in the same transaction, or you will end up paying more in cash out of your own pocket. Use a separate transaction for food items and non-food items, because the store's cash register will only deduct the coupon from your food total and not from the non-food item. Therefore, you will pay more for food items out of your own pocket. For example, you have:

$60 in Food
$20 in Cleaning Supplies

You have **$25** in Food Coupons and **$20** in Cleaning Supplies Coupons = **$45** in coupons

$45 will be deducted from your **$60** food purchase first, totally overlooking the cleaning supplies; therefore, you will pay **$15** on your EBT card. Plus, you would still owe **$20** plus tax in **cash** for the cleaning supplies, totaling $35.00 ($15 EBT and $20 cash.)

Example of Separate Transactions:

EBT only:
$60 in Food
You have **$25** in Food Coupons

$35 will go on your EBT card

Non-Food only:
$20 in Cleaning Supplies
You have **$20** in Cleaning Supplies Coupons

You will only pay the taxes in cash!

Chapter 7

The Art of Couponing

To become a Professional Couponer takes work and a lot of dedication. Now, the true art of a Couponer comes into play when they know when sale ads begin/end, how to stack coupons, and when to buy. Here are a few stores:

Store	Sales Ad Begins	Sales Ad Ends
Publix	Thursday	Wednesday
Target	Sunday	Saturday
Winn-Dixie	Wednesday	Tuesday
Albertsons	Wednesday	Tuesday
Wal-Mart	No Ad	No Ad
Walgreens	Sunday	Saturday
CVS	Sunday	Saturday
Safeway	Wednesday	Tuesday
Wholefoods	Monthly	Monthly
Family Dollar	Wednesday	Tuesday
Kmart	Sunday	Saturday

However, if your store focus is different than mine, find out when their ads begin and end.

Matchups

It's easy to get a matchup cheat sheet, but it's better to learn how to match up your own items. This will help you to become well-versed in finding hidden deals without limiting yourself.

When you start doing your matchups, grab your sales ad, pen, paper and your calculator. When you find an item that appears to be of your liking, go to the coupon database at **thekrazycouponlady.com** or **Southersavers.com**, type in the description of the item in question and the database will pull up a list, like in the example below:

If there are any coupons out there for that particular product:

1. Write it down on your shopping list along with the coupon amount (highest amount), price of the

product, the amount you want to purchase and the price you anticipate paying.

2. Pull the coupons or order your coupons with the highest dollar amount.
3. Plan your shopping route.
4. Pick up your deals.

You can also use your matchup cheat sheet from other websites; however, it's important to look for your own deals as well. They will not find every deal, so it's important to keep your eyes open for bargains, especially on the clearance items. When you find a deal, you need to have an idea of what you should be paying or have an idea of what you should be able to get for free. Throughout my couponing journey, I have found a few items that I usually get for free or pennies on the dollar:

1. Deodorant.
2. Toothpaste.
3. Razors.
4. Glass Cleaner.
5. Cold Medicine.
6. Antacid.
7. Asprin.
8. Soap
9. Salad Dressing.
10. Spaghetti Sauce.
11. Pasta.
12. Rice.

13. Candy.

14. Gum.

And the list goes on. Listed below is a price list that provides a guideline on what I would pay for a bargain.

Item	Bargain Price
Canned Vegetables	Up to $.55
Frozen Dinners	Up to $1.00
Frozen Ice Cream	Up to $2.00
Frozen Pizza	Up to $1.00
Frozen Vegetables	Up to $1.00
Canned Tuna	Up to $.50
Mayonnaise	Up to $1.00
Coffee	Up to $1.50
Cookies	Up to $.75
Crackers	Up to $.75
Peanut Butter	Up to $.75
Juice 64 oz	Up to $1.00
Butter/Margarine	Up to $.50
Cheese	Up to $1.00
Cereal	Up to $1.00
Paper Towels 1 roll	Up to $.75
Bleach	Up to $.75
Laundry Detergent	Up to $1.50
Fabric Softener	Up to $1.00
Toilet Bowl Cleaner	Up to $.75
Trash Bags	Up to $1.50

Soda (12-pack)	Up to $1.00
Body Wash	Up to $1.50
Mouthwash	Up to $1.00

My list is much longer, as you can tell I don't like paying more than a $1 for anything if I don't have to. Paying less than $1.00 is a fair amount to pay; and usually, I end up paying less than that anyway. As you become an experienced couponer, you will have to set your own price limit on products as well. Just remember, what works for one person may not work for the next. Your ultimate goal is to SAVE MONEY period.

Previews

In order to get a heads-up on the coupons, you can log on to SundayCouponPreview.com. Not only are you able to get a sneak peek at the upcoming coupons, but you can also see the previous coupons as well. Once you have your sales ads, you can see if there will be an upcoming coupon in the Sunday's paper or you can determine how many coupons to order from eBay.com, CouponFleaMarket.com, or your coupon clipping service.

Chapter 8

The Breadcrumb 411

As a Couponer, my biggest pet peeve is when retailers run ads, and they do not have the product in stock, especially on the 1st day of the sale. As I became more educated in the tricks of retailers, I have found that some retailers do not restock bargain items for couponers on purpose. Of course, we are able to get a rain check on that item, but the store is banking on us forgetting about it. Their goal is to draw couponers into the store, while creating impulsive shopping in the meantime. Once we are drawn into their store through the sales ad, it's then their job to put up fancy and enticing displays to get us to use other coupons or buy other items that are on sale that we do not have a coupon for.

The sales come from the corporate office, and the store manager does not have any control over what's on sale, but they do have control over whether that product is in stock or not. Some managers will restock their store and some will not just to keep couponers at bay. Walgreens, CVS, and Publix are known for doing this. To my amazement, these 3 stores are well-known for their in-store coupons and the ability for couponers to stack them; but, they are also known for running out of products quickly. Therefore, we must start shopping early, staying on top of the deals, especially when a coupon is close to the expiration date. Although, Publix has stepped up their game in keeping their shelves stocked lately due to the massive complaints; but, I must admit that they are doing better.

The coupon redemption process

Once a week, all stores send their coupons to the corporate office where the person in charge of the coupons will bundle them up and send them to a clearing house for processing. Once receive, the clearinghouse will then separate the coupons, then invoicing the manufacturer for payment. Once the payment is received from the manufacturer, then the store gets their money. Is this a long process? Possibly. It takes the store about 30 days for a complete turnaround. Yes, it's a very tedious process, but grocery stores are not willing to lose out on that money. So, they put out these confusing coupon policies to reduce the likelihood of stockpiling. They know that if you confuse a person who is not well-versed in couponing, they will end up paying more money for their products or giving up altogether. For that reason, I am going to give you the 411 on the major players:

The 411 on Walgreens

At Walgreens, they limit you to 1 coupon per item with a limit of 4 like coupons for the same type of product, which is what they consider as normal household usage; unless a lesser amount is stated on the coupon. They will not allow you to have more coupons than items. For example, you have 8 items with 8 coupons and 2 in-store coupons. Their computer is set up to take 8 coupons for the 8 items. Now in order to use the other 2 in-store coupons, you must add 2 filler items. For my filler items, I simply choose something $.50 or less.

Register Rewards™ (RR)

Walgreens offer great deals using Register Rewards™ every week. However, when using Register Rewards™, it can get a little tricky. For that reason, my goal is to make sure that you are well educated on how this system works.

A Register Rewards™ (RR) is a coupon that prints from a "Catalina" machine after you make a qualifying purchase. Once the transaction is complete, the Catalina machine will print a coupon for "X" amount of  dollars off your next purchase. However, Walgreens will only allow you to receive one RR promotion per product. You can have several different RR promotions, but if you want more of the same item under the same RR promotion—you must do a separate transaction. For example:

You can purchase all of these RR promotions with 1 transaction. If you have manufacturer coupons, you can use them as well.

Earning Register Rewards™

- Register Rewards™ will only print for in-stock merchandise during the promotional period.
- Register Rewards™ can only be earned for eligible items. No substitutions.
- There is a limit of one Register Rewards™ (RR) printed per offer per customer per transaction.
- Customers redeeming a Register Rewards™ against the same offer may not receive another RR.

If you want to purchase 2 RR promotions of the same product—it requires 2 separate transactions.

Once you receive your RR for the 1st transaction, you will not receive the RR on the 2nd transaction if you use your RR from the 1st transaction.

Make sure you use your RR on a different product and manufacturer.

Walgreens has moved to the Balance Rewards system to gain better control over the Redemption process of the Register Rewards. It has become a little tricky, and it has slowed down the couponers tremendously, but the points system is still in place, and it works. It provides less room for people to abuse the system because you must use your Rewards Card; and, it keeps a running list of who is doing what, who is earning what, and what they are redeeming it for. Their system is sort of like that of CVS.

When Redeeming Register Rewards™

- Customers redeeming a Register Rewards™ against the same offer may not receive another RR.
- Refer to Register Rewards™ coupon for expiration date.
- The RR coupon value cannot exceed the total purchase amount. No cash back and no cash value for RR coupon.
- The number of manufacturer coupons, including RR manufacturer coupons, must not exceed the number of items in the transaction.
- Register Rewards™ must be forfeited if the qualifying merchandise is returned.
- Register Rewards™ cannot be used toward the purchase of gift cards and pre-paid cards.
- Register Rewards™ can be redeemed for eligible items only.
- Ineligible items include but are not limited to:
  - Prescriptions
  - Tobacco products
  - Alcoholic beverages
  - Dairy products
  - Lottery tickets
  - Money orders/transfers
  - Transportation passes
  - Special event/entertainment tickets or passes
  - Postage stamps
  - Gift cards/phone cards/prepaid/Green Dot™ cards
  - Prescription Savings Club" memberships
  - Health care services, including immunizations
  - Any items prohibited by law

Register Rewards™ will not print:

1. If the machine is broken. Simply make sure the **green light** is on. If you can't see it, ask the cashier if it's working before you begin checking out.
2. If you bought the wrong product.
3. If you did not meet the purchase amount required. (Example: you must spend $10 and receive $5 in RR.) You must spend $10 and not $9.99.
4. If you use the RR on the same brand of product by the same company. FYI: Sometimes it will print with a different company.

Their Coupon Policy is:

- All valid coupons should be presented to the cashier at the time of checkout.
- Walgreens does not accept expired coupons.
- Coupons and their face value cannot be exchanged for cash or gift cards.
- Competitor coupons are not accepted at Walgreens.
- Walgreens cannot accept coupons for items not carried in our stores.
- The number of manufacturer coupons, including Register Rewards™ manufacturer coupons, may not exceed the number of items in the transaction.

The total value of the coupons may not exceed the value of the transaction. Sales tax must be paid, if required by state law.

- Any coupon offer not covered in these guidelines will be accepted at the discretion of Walgreens management.

Sale Items

- Walgreens will accept manufacturer coupons for an item that is on sale.
- In the event that any item's selling price is less than the value of the coupon, Walgreens will only accept the coupon in exchange for the selling price of the item. Coupon redemption can never exceed the selling price of an item, and no cash back is ever provided in exchange for any coupons.
- Limit 4 coupons per item, unless a lesser amount is stated on the coupon.

Multiple Coupons

- When purchasing a single item, Walgreens accepts one manufacturer coupon and applicable Walgreens coupon(s) for the purchase of a single item, unless prohibited by either coupon offer.
- The coupon amount must be reduced if it exceeds the value of the item after other discounts or coupons are applied. (For example, a $5.00 coupon

for a $4.99 item will result in a $4.99 coupon value).

- When purchasing multiple items, Walgreens accepts multiple identical coupons for multiple qualifying items as long as there is sufficient stock to satisfy other customers, unless a limit is specified. Management reserves the right to limit the quantity of items purchased.

For example: Coupons.com has a coupon for $1.00 off coupon for Listerine and Walgreens has a coupon for $3.00 off Listerine.

Buy 1 Listerine Whitening + Restoring (16-oz.) at $4.99 each
Use 1 $1/1 Listerine printable coupon from coupons.com
Stack with $3/1 coupon in the weekly sales flier
(deducting $4)

After coupons, you will pay $1.99 for Listerine (don't forget your filler item of $.50 or less, you have 2 coupons for 1 product.)

Buy One, Get One Free Coupons

- When items are featured in a Buy One, Get One Free promotion, up to two coupons can be used against the items being purchased, as long as the net price does not go below zero for the items being purchased.
- Sales tax must be paid for any Buy One, Get One Free coupon offers, if required by applicable state laws.

The 411 on CVS

At CVS, rewards are called **ExtraCare Bucks (ECB)**, you can earn ECB's at any CVS/pharmacy store or online when you use your ExtraCare card. Yes, you must sign up for this card. An individual cannot have more than one card, but another member of

your family can have their own card—they are tracked by the phone number on each card.

CVS registers are set to allow 1 CVS coupon and 1 manufacturer coupon per item. As a matter of fact, their ExtraCare Bucks are redeemed like a gift card, not a coupon. They can be combined with store and manufacturer coupons; however they cannot be used to pay tax. It's much easier than Walgreens; however, they are strict on their limits. CVS limit some items to one per household—which means, one per promotion per CVS rewards card. When redeeming your ExtraCare Bucks, the bucks must match the card that you made the qualifying purchase on. Therefore, you need to make sure to keep your ExtraCare Bucks separate if you are maintaining more than one card.

If the coupon does not scan, CVS will not accept your coupon. CVS does not accept any expired coupons, including expired ExtraCare Bucks. All coupons must match the product being purchased; they do not "double" or "triple" coupons or allow overage. If you buy an item for $.75, and you have a $1.00 off coupon, the cashier will adjust your coupon to $.75.

Free coupons or "offers at the register" (OAR's) are unearned and issued to you as a valued member of the CVS/pharmacy ExtraCare program. These coupons take the form of "open ended" coupons such as $3 off $15 or a certain dollar amount off a specific item. In any given transaction their registers will allow only **one "open ended" coupon per transaction.** However, ExtraCare bucks are earned when you make a qualifying purchase; and are not limited like the OAR's.

BOGO

In the case where a particular item is on sale for "buy one get one free" (BOGO), you are only allowed to use one manufacturer's BOGO coupon. For instance, if Revlon lipstick is on sale for BOGO, you can use one manufacturer's BOGO coupon. You would get both items free and pay any applicable tax. However, they reserve the right to limit quantities on all items. If CVS is running a sale for BOGO, you can use two manufacturer coupons for a specific dollar amount off. For example, if Revlon lipstick is on sale at our store for BOGO, you can use two $1.00 off Revlon lipstick manufacturer coupons.

The 411 on Publix

Publix is known for having some of the best deals; however, what sets them apart from the rest is their Publix Promise:

Our PUBLIX checkout PROMISE guarantees that if during checkout, the scanned price of an item (excluding alcohol and tobacco products) exceeds the shelf price or advertised price, we will give the customer one of that item free. The remaining items will be charged at the lower price.

Keeping the Publix promise is one thing; but, Publix had an even bigger issue about each store having a different coupon policy. As Publix loyal customers and couponers began to complain—they started listening. Not only had that, due to the increase in coupon usage, the store managers began complaining about the couponers. Now my question is, "How can you complain about couponers when you put out so many coupons?" Regardless of the great deals, questions or complaints—Publix decided to streamline their coupon policy:

Publix accepts manufacturer coupons (limit one per item), Publix coupons (originals only—no copies), valid Internet coupons, and coupons from nearby competitors identified by each Publix store. (Competitor names are posted at each Publix store.) We will accept coupons from competing pharmacies for prescriptions only. We will not accept percent-off-items or percent-off-total-order coupons. We will only accept coupons for identical merchandise we sell. Acceptance is subject to any restrictions on the coupon, and we reserve the right to limit quantities. Manager approval is needed for individual coupons above $5.00. For a buy-one-get-one free (BOGO) offer, each item is considered a separate sale. We will accept a manufacturer's coupon and either a Publix or a competitor coupon on the same item. Dollars-off-total-order coupons will be limited to one Publix and one competitor coupon per order. The order total must be equal to or greater than the total purchase requirements indicated on the coupon(s) presented.

I have received a lot of free items because I pay attention to my prices and so can you. I have found the greatest deals in Heath/Beauty & Food Advantage Flyers.

You can find these 2 coupon booklets along with the sales ad at Publix's main entrance on a swivel rack. Don't forget that you can use 1 manufacturer's coupon and one in store coupon—so, pay attention to the monthly deals.

Some Publix stores are limiting Publix coupons to 1-4 deals per customer, 4 BOGO deals per customer or 8 coupons per item, unless a lesser amount is stated on the coupon. When shopping at Publix, find out what their limits are on the coupons before shopping. This will save you a lot of time. Although Publix promotes stocking up on sale items, they will not tell you about the limits in advance—they allow you to fill your cart up and then limit you once you get to the register. So it behooves you to know the limits in advance to ensure that you are able to plan accordingly.

Publix will not price-match, but they will double any manufacturer's coupon that is $0.50 or less in some states, but definitely not in Alabama and Florida.

The 411 on Target

Target is one of the least complicated stores—they keep everything real simple.

- Target accepts one manufacturer coupon and one Target coupon for the same item with a limit of 4.
- Super Target coupons can be used in any Target store if the store carries the item.
- Target will gladly accept valid internet coupons.
- Target will accept two kinds of coupons: Target-issued coupons and manufacturer-issued.

- Target will accept one Target coupon and one manufacturer coupon for the same item, unless either coupon prohibits it.

- Coupon amount may be reduced if it exceeds the value of the item after other discounts or coupons are applied.

- Target will not give cash back if the face value of a coupon is greater than the purchase value of the item.

- Target will not accept coupons from other retailers, or coupons for products not carried in our stores.

In order to get coupons from Target, go to their website at Target.com.

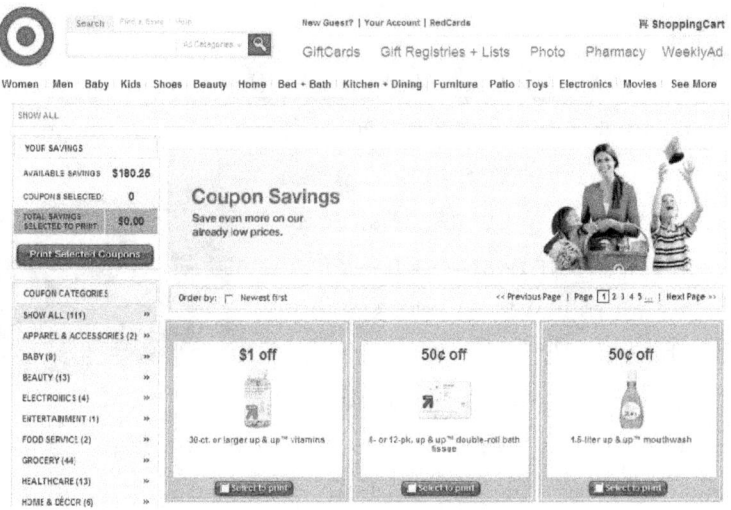

Usually, new coupons are posted every Sunday. Even if you don't need a coupon right now, print it out. Target coupons can hit their print limit very quickly. So don't drag your feet when it comes down to printing out your coupons.

Mobile Coupons

Target will send mobile coupons to your web-enabled phone up to five times a month via text message. When you get ready to redeem your mobile coupon, just show the barcode to the cashier, and they will scan it applying your savings instantly. Sign up at Target.com.

The 411 on Winn-Dixie

You must have a Winn-Dixie Reward card to get the discounted or sale price. You can sign up at any Winn-Dixie store or online at Winn-Dixie.com.

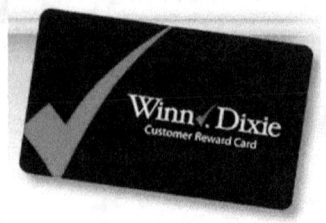

Randomly Winn-Dixie Catalina machine will print a $10/50 coupon that you are able to use during the next week. So, watch out for your coupon, plus you are able to use that same Catalina coupon at Publix if Winn-Dixie is considered one of their competitors.

Winn-Dixie coupon policy is real easy. They will take:

- One manufacturer coupon and one Winn-Dixie coupon for the same item.
- Valid internet coupons.
- One coupon for each BOGO item. Basically, you are able to use a total of 2 manufacturer coupons on a BOGO item.

Although, Winn-Dixie doesn't price match, they are stepping up their game with their in-store coupons. They are dropping their prices, and some stores are trying to take competitors coupons; but, it gets very tricky from store to store depending on the store manager.

The 411 on Wal-Mart

Wal-Mart is the best with price-matching. They will price-match any item that you find at another store at a lower price. The "Ad Match Guarantee" states:

We're committed to providing low prices every day. On everything. So if you find a lower advertised price on an identical product, tell us and we'll match it. Right at the register.

They will gladly match the price in the following types of ads:

- Buy one, get one free ad with a specified price for example: Buy one for $2.49, get one free (BOGO)
- Competitor's ads that feature a specific item for a specified price.
- Preferred shopping card prices for specific items that are in a printed ad.
- For fresh produce and meat items when the price is offered in the same unit type (lb. for lb.; each for each)

Items purchased must be identical to the ad (size, quantity, brand, flavor, color, etc.

Wal-Mart does not honor:

- Ads when the actual price for items cannot be determined.
- Internet pricing
- Misprinted ad prices of other retailers
- "Going out of business" sales or "close out" prices
- Percentage off sale

Wal-Mart Coupon Policy

- Print-at-home internet coupons
  - Must be legible
  - Must have "Manufacturer Coupon" printed on them

- o Must have a valid remit address for the manufacturer
- o Must have a valid expiration date
- o Must have a scannable bar code
- o Buy one, get one free (BOGO) coupons with a specified price
- o Are acceptable in black and white or color
- o May not be duplicated
- Manufacturer coupons
  - o For dollar/cents off
  - o For free items (except those printed off the Internet)
  - o Buy one, get one free (BOGO) coupons
  - o Must have "Manufacturer Coupon" printed on them
  - o Must have a valid remit address for the manufacturer
  - o Must have a valid expiration date
  - o Must have a scannable bar code
  - o May not be duplicated
- Competitor's coupons
  - o A specific item for a specified price, for example, $2.99 for Charmin Toilet Paper
  - o Buy one, get one free (BOGO) coupons for items **with** a specified price
  - o Have a valid expiration date

- o Are acceptable in black and white
- Soft drink container caps
- Checkout coupons ("Catalinas")
  - o Printed at our competitors' registers for dollar/cents off on a specific item
  - o Must have "Manufacturer Coupon" with specific item requirements printed on them
  - o Must have a valid remit address for the manufacturer
  - o Must have a valid expiration date
  - o Must have a scannable bar code
  - o Are acceptable in black and white
  - o May not be duplicated

Wal-Mart DOES NOT accept the following coupons:

- Checkout coupons
  - o Dollars/cents off the entire basket purchase
  - o Percentage off the entire basket purchase
- Print-at-home Internet coupons that require no purchase
- Competitor's coupons
  - o Dollars/cents off at a specific retailer
  - o Percentage off
  - o Buy one, get one free (BOGO) coupons **without** a specified price

o   Double- or triple-value coupons

The following are guidelines and limitations:

- They only accept coupons for merchandise that they sell.
- Coupons must be presented at the time of purchase.
- Only one coupon per item.
- Item purchased must be identical to the coupon (size, quantity, brand, flavor, color, etc.).
- There is no limit on the number of coupons per transaction.
- Coupons must have an expiration date and be redeemed prior to expiration.
- If coupon value exceeds the price of the item, the excess may be given to the customer as cash or applied toward the basket purchase.
- SNAP items purchased in a SNAP transaction are ineligible for cash back.
- WIC items purchased in a WIC transaction are applied to the basket purchase and may not be eligible for cash back. Refer to state-specific WIC guidelines.
- Great Value, Marketside, Equate, Parents Choice, and World Table coupons have no cash value and

are ineligible for cash back or application to the basket purchase.

- The system will prompt for supervisor verification for:
    - 40 coupons per transaction.
    - A coupon of $20 or greater on one item.
    - $50 or more in coupons in one transaction.

Wal-Mart's coupon policy is located on their website at Walmart.com.

Chapter 9

Coupon Discrimination

Does discrimination exist when it comes down to using coupons? The answer is yes. There is discrimination in everything that we do—everyone has an opinion, and couponing is no different. I experience coupon discrimination all the time, but it does not stop me from saving money. I control my finances, I control my mental state, I control what I put in my body, and the opinions of others do not bother me if they choose not to become a good steward over what God has blessed them with!

When you really master using coupons and start saving some real money, you will find that cashiers and managers begin to critique the way you are using coupons. They will actually look for reasons to reject a coupon in order for you to pay more than you have to. Therefore, it is imperative that you make sure that you read your coupons carefully and use them for the correct item.

Manufacturers spend a lot of their marketing dollars promoting their product through the use of coupons. They bank on their coupons inducing consumers to buy products that they would not buy otherwise. In so many words, a manufacturer would prefer to sell 10,000 products with a coupon, than selling 4,000 products without a coupon. So, make sure you are reading your coupons carefully to ensure you are getting the right item.

The Truth behind the Discrimination

Whenever we use a coupon, the store does not receive their money up front. It takes about 30 days for them to receive the funds for the products purchased with a coupon; therefore, the store does not get credit for the actual sale. They receive credit for the cash, credit card and EBT purchases; plus, it does affect the bonus structure of the Managerial staff if there are more couponers than actual customers.

If a store feels as if you are saving too much money and they cannot make a profit from you—then they make it difficult for you, in hopes that you find another location to shop. I have personally experienced this happening most often at select Publix stores in the Central Florida and Alabama stores that are hit hard by couponers. Some Publix stores are coupon friendly, and there are some that will make your life a living nightmare—if that happens, find another store that you are comfortable with.

Coupon Deception

By now, we should already know that the manufacturer creates coupons for their products to get us, as consumers, to buy what we would not buy otherwise. Therefore, we end up spending more than we plan to spend blowing our budget, when we should be trying to save money. However, this only happens to those who are not well versed in coupon usage or those who fall prey to coupon discrimination. Of course, like all things, couponing is a numbers game. If you are not focused on finding a bargain, you will end up spending more than you are saving. Believe it or not, the manufacturer's bank on the inexperienced people to use coupons to buy or try their products to get them hooked on that particular product.

Now is the time to master the couponing game, it is time for you to learn how to really save some real money. Just because you have a coupon for an item does not mean that you must buy it, unless it's a bargain. The goal of a Coupon Expert is to find bargains and not a discount—we can find discounts anywhere; but, a bargain must be sought after. So, forget about coupon discrimination and learn how to save yourself some real money. That means that we must do our homework and find the hidden treasures that the manufacturers and stores leave behind.

Chapter 10

Share Your Breadcrumbs!

As a Coupon Expert, you must learn your prices and just because an ad says that an item is on sale does not mean that it's a deal. If you don't have at least two coupons to stack to create your own deal, then you must know your prices to prevent yourself from getting duped. A real Couponer chooses between using a coupon or spending more of his or her money. If you like having money in your pocket, you should consider using coupons to save your money. If you like giving, you should consider using coupons to give as well.

Once you master how to use coupons, your cupboard will never be empty. There is so much free food in your local grocery store; you would not believe. It has been said that 2% of the coupons actually get redeemed. Why is that? Most people, who claim to be busy, don't have time to clip coupons and save money, but somehow they find time to watch television, talk on the phone, or engaging in activities that are costing them money opposed to saving money.

You will find that those who spend more money will have less of it at the end of the day. Those who spend less of their money will have more of it at the end of the day. I am saying all of that to say this—use coupons as a replacement for spending your hard earned dollar bills. You will find that you are better able to afford the things that people are crying about not having. As a Couponer, you will also find that when you exercise wisdom in your finances—you become a good steward over what you have and do not have in life.

Give to those in need

If you cannot afford to give to your community, couponing opens a door for you to do so. Most often, we find a good deal, and that good deal is still sitting on the shelf unopened. What a waste! A good deal is not a good deal if it's left unused. Find a use for the bargains that you find—there are many people who would love to have what's sitting around your house gathering dust. Once you become an expert, consider donating your extra items to charity, they will gladly take your donations.

I have found that the more I give, the more I receive. I am still amazed at the bargains that I find and the way God has enabled me to become blessed and be a blessing to others. Now, that you have this vital information about couponing—what you do from this point on is up to you. Be Blessed and be a Blessing to Someone Else.

Coupon Breadcrumbs

Where to find coupons:

1. Coupons.com
2. SmartSource.com
3. RedPlum.com
4. Target.com
5. Store websites
6. Manufacturer's website
7. All You Magazine (Wal-Mart Only)

What website to use to look for deals or to create a shopping list:

1. Thekrazycouponlady.com
2. Southersavers.com
3. Iheartpublix.com (Publix Shoppers)
4. www.totallytarget.com (Target Shoppers)

What Coupon Clipping Service can I use?

1. eBay.com
2. CouponFleaMarket.com
3. CollectableCoupons.com
4. TheCouponClippers.com

"The work is already done; all you have to do is find it!"

The Breadcrumb Series: Don't Miss Out!

Send The Breadcrumb Series Testimonies,
Donations, or Orders to
Ruby Fleurcius
581 N. Park Ave. Ste. #725
Apopka, FL 32704
321-312-0744
RubyFleurcius@BreadcrumbSeries.com

Books are $14.95 each. Please mail checks or
money orders. Credit Card or PayPal orders
are online.

The Couponing Breadcrumb's Shopping List

Day: _____ Date: _____

Store: _____

Item	CPN
1.	
2.	
3.	
4.	
5.	
6.	
7.	
8.	
9.	
10.	
11.	
12.	
13.	
14.	
15.	
16.	
17.	
18.	
19.	
20.	
21.	
22.	
23.	
24.	
25.	

The Couponing Breadcrumb's Shopping List

Day: _____ *Date:* _____

Store: _____

Item	CPN
1.	
2.	
3.	
4.	
5.	
6.	
7.	
8.	
9.	
10.	
11.	
12.	
13.	
14.	
15.	
16.	
17.	
18.	
19.	
20.	
21.	
22.	
23.	
24.	
25.	

The Couponing Breadcrumb's Shopping List

Day: _____ Date: _____

Store: _____

Item	CPN
1.	
2.	
3.	
4.	
5.	
6.	
7.	
8.	
9.	
10.	
11.	
12.	
13.	
14.	
15.	
16.	
17.	
18.	
19.	
20.	
21.	
22.	
23.	
24.	
25.	

The Couponing Breadcrumb's Shopping List

Day: _____ *Date:* _____

Store: _____

Item	CPN
1.	
2.	
3.	
4.	
5.	
6.	
7.	
8.	
9.	
10.	
11.	
12.	
13.	
14.	
15.	
16.	
17.	
18.	
19.	
20.	
21.	
22.	
23.	
24.	
25.	

The Couponing Breadcrumb's Shopping List

Day: _____   Date: _____

Store: _____

Item	CPN
1.	
2.	
3.	
4.	
5.	
6.	
7.	
8.	
9.	
10.	
11.	
12.	
13.	
14.	
15.	
16.	
17.	
18.	
19.	
20.	
21.	
22.	
23.	
24.	
25.	

The Couponing Breadcrumb's Shopping List

Day: _____ Date: _____

Store: _____

Item	CPN
1.	
2.	
3.	
4.	
5.	
6.	
7.	
8.	
9.	
10.	
11.	
12.	
13.	
14.	
15.	
16.	
17.	
18.	
19.	
20.	
21.	
22.	
23.	
24.	
25.	

The Couponing Breadcrumb's Shopping List

Day: _____ Date: _____

Store: _____

Item	CPN
1.	
2.	
3.	
4.	
5.	
6.	
7.	
8.	
9.	
10.	
11.	
12.	
13.	
14.	
15.	
16.	
17.	
18.	
19.	
20.	
21.	
22.	
23.	
24.	
25.	

The Couponing Breadcrumb's Shopping List

Day: _____ Date: _____

Store: _____

Item	CPN
1.	
2.	
3.	
4.	
5.	
6.	
7.	
8.	
9.	
10.	
11.	
12.	
13.	
14.	
15.	
16.	
17.	
18.	
19.	
20.	
21.	
22.	
23.	
24.	
25.	

The Couponing Breadcrumb's
Shopping List

Day: _____ *Date:* _____

Store: _____

Item	CPN
1.	
2.	
3.	
4.	
5.	
6.	
7.	
8.	
9.	
10.	
11.	
12.	
13.	
14.	
15.	
16.	
17.	
18.	
19.	
20.	
21.	
22.	
23.	
24.	
25.	

The Couponing Breadcrumb's
Shopping List

Day: _____ *Date:* _____

Store: _____

Item	CPN
1.	
2.	
3.	
4.	
5.	
6.	
7.	
8.	
9.	
10.	
11.	
12.	
13.	
14.	
15.	
16.	
17.	
18.	
19.	
20.	
21.	
22.	
23.	
24.	
25.	

The Couponing Breadcrumb's
Shopping List

Day: _____ *Date:* _____

Store: _____

Item	CPN
1.	
2.	
3.	
4.	
5.	
6.	
7.	
8.	
9.	
10.	
11.	
12.	
13.	
14.	
15.	
16.	
17.	
18.	
19.	
20.	
21.	
22.	
23.	
24.	
25.	

The Couponing Breadcrumb's
Shopping List

Day: _____ *Date:* _____

Store: _____

Item	CPN
1.	
2.	
3.	
4.	
5.	
6.	
7.	
8.	
9.	
10.	
11.	
12.	
13.	
14.	
15.	
16.	
17.	
18.	
19.	
20.	
21.	
22.	
23.	
24.	
25.	

The Couponing Breadcrumb's
Shopping List

Day: _____ Date: _____

Store: _____

Item	CPN
1.	
2.	
3.	
4.	
5.	
6.	
7.	
8.	
9.	
10.	
11.	
12.	
13.	
14.	
15.	
16.	
17.	
18.	
19.	
20.	
21.	
22.	
23.	
24.	
25.	

The Couponing Breadcrumb's
Shopping List

Day: _____ *Date:* _____

Store: _____

Item	CPN
1.	
2.	
3.	
4.	
5.	
6.	
7.	
8.	
9.	
10.	
11.	
12.	
13.	
14.	
15.	
16.	
17.	
18.	
19.	
20.	
21.	
22.	
23.	
24.	
25.	

The Couponing Breadcrumb's Shopping List

Day: _____ Date: _____

Store: _____

Item	CPN
1.	
2.	
3.	
4.	
5.	
6.	
7.	
8.	
9.	
10.	
11.	
12.	
13.	
14.	
15.	
16.	
17.	
18.	
19.	
20.	
21.	
22.	
23.	
24.	
25.	

The Couponing Breadcrumb's
Shopping List

Day: _____ *Date:* _____

Store: _____

Item	CPN
1.	
2.	
3.	
4.	
5.	
6.	
7.	
8.	
9.	
10.	
11.	
12.	
13.	
14.	
15.	
16.	
17.	
18.	
19.	
20.	
21.	
22.	
23.	
24.	
25.	

The Couponing Breadcrumb's Shopping List

Day: _____ Date: _____

Store: _____

Item	CPN
1.	
2.	
3.	
4.	
5.	
6.	
7.	
8.	
9.	
10.	
11.	
12.	
13.	
14.	
15.	
16.	
17.	
18.	
19.	
20.	
21.	
22.	
23.	
24.	
25.	

The Couponing Breadcrumb's Shopping List

Day: _____ Date: _____

Store: _____

Item	CPN
1.	
2.	
3.	
4.	
5.	
6.	
7.	
8.	
9.	
10.	
11.	
12.	
13.	
14.	
15.	
16.	
17.	
18.	
19.	
20.	
21.	
22.	
23.	
24.	
25.	

The Couponing Breadcrumb's Shopping List

Day: _____ Date: _____

Store: _____

Item	CPN
1.	
2.	
3.	
4.	
5.	
6.	
7.	
8.	
9.	
10.	
11.	
12.	
13.	
14.	
15.	
16.	
17.	
18.	
19.	
20.	
21.	
22.	
23.	
24.	
25.	

The Couponing Breadcrumb's Shopping List

Day: _____ *Date:* _____

Store: _____

Item	CPN
1.	
2.	
3.	
4.	
5.	
6.	
7.	
8.	
9.	
10.	
11.	
12.	
13.	
14.	
15.	
16.	
17.	
18.	
19.	
20.	
21.	
22.	
23.	
24.	
25.	

The Couponing Breadcrumb's Shopping List

Day: _____ Date: _____

Store: _____

Item	CPN
1.	
2.	
3.	
4.	
5.	
6.	
7.	
8.	
9.	
10.	
11.	
12.	
13.	
14.	
15.	
16.	
17.	
18.	
19.	
20.	
21.	
22.	
23.	
24.	
25.	

The Couponing Breadcrumb's Shopping List

Day: _____ Date: _____

Store: _____

Item	CPN
1.	
2.	
3.	
4.	
5.	
6.	
7.	
8.	
9.	
10.	
11.	
12.	
13.	
14.	
15.	
16.	
17.	
18.	
19.	
20.	
21.	
22.	
23.	
24.	
25.	

The Couponing Breadcrumb's Shopping List

Day: _____ Date: _____

Store: _____

Item	CPN
1.	
2.	
3.	
4.	
5.	
6.	
7.	
8.	
9.	
10.	
11.	
12.	
13.	
14.	
15.	
16.	
17.	
18.	
19.	
20.	
21.	
22.	
23.	
24.	
25.	

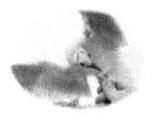

The Couponing Breadcrumb's Shopping List

Day: _____   *Date:* _____

Store: _____

Item	CPN
1.	
2.	
3.	
4.	
5.	
6.	
7.	
8.	
9.	
10.	
11.	
12.	
13.	
14.	
15.	
16.	
17.	
18.	
19.	
20.	
21.	
22.	
23.	
24.	
25.	

The Couponing Breadcrumb's Shopping List

Day: _____ Date: _____

Store: _____

Item	CPN
1.	
2.	
3.	
4.	
5.	
6.	
7.	
8.	
9.	
10.	
11.	
12.	
13.	
14.	
15.	
16.	
17.	
18.	
19.	
20.	
21.	
22.	
23.	
24.	
25.	

The Couponing Breadcrumb's Shopping List

Day: _____ *Date:* _____

Store: _____

Item	CPN
1.	
2.	
3.	
4.	
5.	
6.	
7.	
8.	
9.	
10.	
11.	
12.	
13.	
14.	
15.	
16.	
17.	
18.	
19.	
20.	
21.	
22.	
23.	
24.	
25.	

The Couponing Breadcrumb's Shopping List

Day: _____ Date: _____

Store: _____

	Item	CPN
1.		
2.		
3.		
4.		
5.		
6.		
7.		
8.		
9.		
10.		
11.		
12.		
13.		
14.		
15.		
16.		
17.		
18.		
19.		
20.		
21.		
22.		
23.		
24.		
25.		

The Couponing Breadcrumb's Shopping List

Day: _____ *Date:* _____

Store: _____

Item	CPN
1.	
2.	
3.	
4.	
5.	
6.	
7.	
8.	
9.	
10.	
11.	
12.	
13.	
14.	
15.	
16.	
17.	
18.	
19.	
20.	
21.	
22.	
23.	
24.	
25.	

The Couponing Breadcrumb's Shopping List

Day: _____ Date: _____

Store: _____

Item	CPN
1.	
2.	
3.	
4.	
5.	
6.	
7.	
8.	
9.	
10.	
11.	
12.	
13.	
14.	
15.	
16.	
17.	
18.	
19.	
20.	
21.	
22.	
23.	
24.	
25.	

The Couponing Breadcrumb's
Shopping List

Day: _____ *Date:* _____

Store: _____

Item	CPN
1.	
2.	
3.	
4.	
5.	
6.	
7.	
8.	
9.	
10.	
11.	
12.	
13.	
14.	
15.	
16.	
17.	
18.	
19.	
20.	
21.	
22.	
23.	
24.	
25.	

The Couponing Breadcrumb's Shopping List

Day: _____ Date: _____

Store: _____

Item	CPN
1.	
2.	
3.	
4.	
5.	
6.	
7.	
8.	
9.	
10.	
11.	
12.	
13.	
14.	
15.	
16.	
17.	
18.	
19.	
20.	
21.	
22.	
23.	
24.	
25.	

The Couponing Breadcrumb's
Shopping List

Day: _____ *Date:* _____

Store: _____

Item	CPN
1.	
2.	
3.	
4.	
5.	
6.	
7.	
8.	
9.	
10.	
11.	
12.	
13.	
14.	
15.	
16.	
17.	
18.	
19.	
20.	
21.	
22.	
23.	
24.	
25.	

The Couponing Breadcrumb's Shopping List

Day: _____ Date: _____

Store: _____

Item	CPN
1.	
2.	
3.	
4.	
5.	
6.	
7.	
8.	
9.	
10.	
11.	
12.	
13.	
14.	
15.	
16.	
17.	
18.	
19.	
20.	
21.	
22.	
23.	
24.	
25.	

The Couponing Breadcrumb's Shopping List

Day: _____ *Date:* _____

Store: _____

Item	CPN
1.	
2.	
3.	
4.	
5.	
6.	
7.	
8.	
9.	
10.	
11.	
12.	
13.	
14.	
15.	
16.	
17.	
18.	
19.	
20.	
21.	
22.	
23.	
24.	
25.	

The Couponing Breadcrumb's Shopping List

Day: _____   Date: _____

Store: _____

Item	CPN
1.	
2.	
3.	
4.	
5.	
6.	
7.	
8.	
9.	
10.	
11.	
12.	
13.	
14.	
15.	
16.	
17.	
18.	
19.	
20.	
21.	
22.	
23.	
24.	
25.	

The Couponing Breadcrumb's
Shopping List

Day: _____ *Date:* _____

Store: _____

Item	CPN
1.	
2.	
3.	
4.	
5.	
6.	
7.	
8.	
9.	
10.	
11.	
12.	
13.	
14.	
15.	
16.	
17.	
18.	
19.	
20.	
21.	
22.	
23.	
24.	
25.	

The Couponing Breadcrumb's Shopping List

Day: _____ *Date:* _____

Store: _____

Item	CPN
1.	
2.	
3.	
4.	
5.	
6.	
7.	
8.	
9.	
10.	
11.	
12.	
13.	
14.	
15.	
16.	
17.	
18.	
19.	
20.	
21.	
22.	
23.	
24.	
25.	

The Couponing Breadcrumb's
Shopping List

Day: _____ *Date:* _____

Store: _____

Item	CPN
1.	
2.	
3.	
4.	
5.	
6.	
7.	
8.	
9.	
10.	
11.	
12.	
13.	
14.	
15.	
16.	
17.	
18.	
19.	
20.	
21.	
22.	
23.	
24.	
25.	

The Couponing Breadcrumb's
Shopping List

Day: _____ Date: _____

Store: _____

	Item	CPN
1.		
2.		
3.		
4.		
5.		
6.		
7.		
8.		
9.		
10.		
11.		
12.		
13.		
14.		
15.		
16.		
17.		
18.		
19.		
20.		
21.		
22.		
23.		
24.		
25.		

The Couponing Breadcrumb's Shopping List

Day: _____ *Date:* _____

Store: _____

Item	CPN
1.	
2.	
3.	
4.	
5.	
6.	
7.	
8.	
9.	
10.	
11.	
12.	
13.	
14.	
15.	
16.	
17.	
18.	
19.	
20.	
21.	
22.	
23.	
24.	
25.	

The Couponing Breadcrumb's Shopping List

Day: _____ Date: _____

Store: _____

Item	CPN
1.	
2.	
3.	
4.	
5.	
6.	
7.	
8.	
9.	
10.	
11.	
12.	
13.	
14.	
15.	
16.	
17.	
18.	
19.	
20.	
21.	
22.	
23.	
24.	
25.	

The Couponing Breadcrumb's Shopping List

Day: _____   Date: _____

Store: _____

Item	CPN
1.	
2.	
3.	
4.	
5.	
6.	
7.	
8.	
9.	
10.	
11.	
12.	
13.	
14.	
15.	
16.	
17.	
18.	
19.	
20.	
21.	
22.	
23.	
24.	
25.